Purposed Students

A Guide to Being Great

Written by Dr. Michael A. Winters

Text Copyright © 2018 by Dr. Michael A. Winters

All rights reserved. This book or any portion thereof may not be reproduced or used in any manner whatsoever without the express written permission of the publisher - except for the use of brief quotations in a book review or article.

Published in the United States by

MLR, LLC

Vicksburg, MS

First Printing 2018

ISBN 10: 0999892312

ISBN 13: 978-0999892312

wwwMLRmasterpieces.com

Purposed Students

A Guide to Being Great

Written by Dr. Michael A. Winters

Part A – The Dream

Introduction

What if I told you that you could be ten times better than what you currently are by making simple changes consistently over time? That's the question that I ask people all the time and generally get the same response. You know, the look that says - yeah right, or really, go on and amuse me. Others immediately respond with what's the catch. There is no catch, and this is not a gimmick. It is simply a matter of focus and discipline. The truth of the matter is just saying that you will **only** get ten times better is an understatement.

People are so accustomed to getting everything done in an instant and seeking immediate results that they miss what develops into something powerful over time. I like to reference a watermelon seed. That tiny watermelon seed which is as small as your fingertip has the capability of becoming exponentially greater than its initial size. In fact, it can grow from the size of your fingertip to weighing ten to fifteen pounds. Why does that particular seed become a watermelon? Because of everything within the seed that says *"let me out*! I am so much more than what I am currently". So, I say that you must have the tenacity of a watermelon seed that's planted in the soil. Multiple things happen to that seed while it is in the soil that is never seen by the naked eye. Here's my point, you can become exponentially better on the inside long before anyone on the outside sees what you have been working on in your life. During the process (known as germination in this case) the seed is filled with things that may not appear to be appealing, but it is going through the most powerful aspect of it's planted life. I like to use this as my reference when I talk to people about being "purposed students."

Characteristics of a Purposed Student

Purposed students know that they exist for a reason and they succeed at what they do. In other words, they may not know exactly why they exist, but there is a yearning within their hearts that declare: I am better than what I see right now. I know that I matter, I know that I can make positive contributions, I know that given the proper guidance and resources, I can achieve.

Becoming a purposed student is a process that takes time and deliberate effort to not settle for being average or operating beneath your potential. Enduring that process is what separates the haves, and the have-nots, the winners and the quitters, the successful and the unsuccessful, the innovative and the mundane. This guide is designed to help you navigate the process and help you to become a "purposed student." It is part of the coaching program that enables you to move from where you are to where you want to be. ***I do have to warn you that completing this with all of your heart and with a focused attitude will wreck every fiber of mediocrity, lack, and lazy bone in your body!*** You will find yourself excelling to new heights that you never thought imaginable. You will accomplish goals that you never thought possible and become a compelling success story!

A "Purposed Student" has goals, dreams, and aspirations.

Goals, dreams, and aspirations are all related but slightly different. Dreams and aspirations are siblings while goals are their first cousin.

Goals, for example, are merely measurable plans to achieve something. Example: My goal is to save $5,000.00 in a year. Another example: My goal is to lose ten pounds in six weeks.

Dreams, on the other hand, are things that you know do not exist at the current time, are currently out of reach, but you hope and believe that they will come true. Example: Dr. Martin Luther King, Jr. stated in his famous I Have a Dream Speech - "I have a dream that my four little children will one day live in a nation where they will not be judged by the color of their skin but by the content of their character." This speech occurred during one of the darkest times in American history. Dreams are what require goals and aspirations to get to the destination.

Aspirations are things that you desire that are within reach but will take achieving multiple goals to get there.

Goals, dreams, and aspirations are so dynamic once they are combined with deliberate effort, become rocket fuel for your success. They help you to understand more clearly why you exist. Here's a tip - your reason for living exists in little clues all around you. They exist in things that make you happy, things that make you angry, desires that you have regarding particular issues, problems that you solve more easily than others. The key to becoming successful in accomplishing goals, reaching aspirations and fulfilling dreams is locked in those clues. I want to help you unlock those clues. Do you have the desire to move forward? Are you willing to spend time going through the process? If so, let's continue!

You Exist for a Reason

So why do you exist? It's okay if you do not know at the moment. The next few activities will help you to discover some clues along the way. Keep in mind the example of the watermelon seed that saw earlier. The key to its survival in the soil is its inner cry - "*Let me out! I am more than this.*" What is screaming out on the inside of you? What do you feel that you can make a difference in if all of the conditions were favorable for you?

Here is a quick example of what I am talking about- As a child, I always wanted the people that I cared about to get along without arguing and tearing each other down. I didn't know why it would bother me so much to hear people talk about others behind their backs. It turns out that one of my greatest gifts is to help people relationally. Another example, I've always been drawn towards gifted speakers, I could sit and listen for hours to people who just had the gift to communicate in speaking. Growing up as a kid I used to cut grass with my father and we also cleaned law offices. I used to imagine what it would be like to live in the house of a doctor or a lawyer and picture myself "making it big" or making something successful of myself. I never really thought that I could be in that position based on my experiences at that time. However, I had the opportunity to be exposed as I grew older to certain people who helped me along the way. Little did I know that those thoughts and dreams that I had were clues to where I needed to focus. I've always wanted to make a difference in somebody's life even as a child.

I want you to answer the next series of questions regarding your dreams. No one but you will have access to these answers unless you choose to share them. Sometimes it is difficult to share your dreams with others because they may not be able to relate. That is okay if they don't. After all, it's **your** dream. When you answer these questions, I want you to be thoughtful, take your time, and not rush through these just to get finished - remember the cycle of the watermelon seed? It takes time and deliberate effort to become successful.

1. Describe the most important achievement that you have made to date? Explain why this was important to you.

This achievement doesn't necessarily have to be regarding educational attainment. It is merely something that you recently did that makes you proud. It does not have only to focus on academics.

_____
_____
_____
_____
_____
_____
_____
_____
_____
_____
_____
_____
_____
_____
_____

2. Tell me about times that you dreamed of accomplishing something or doing something great in your life (in other words, what's your wildest dream of accomplishment right now.)
Be as descriptive and vivid as you can.

Note: This particular question will require careful thinking.

_____
_____
_____
_____
_____
_____
_____
_____
_____
_____
_____
_____
_____
_____
_____

3. If you could accomplish this dream, what would it take to get there? How realistic is this dream?
What barriers would be in your way?

_____
_____
_____
_____
_____
_____
_____
_____
_____
_____
_____
_____
_____
_____
_____
_____

4. Who do you know or know of that is already living your dream?

Note: It may be helpful to reflect on a person who had made it when the odds were against them. If you know them personally, arrange a time to talk to them and tell them that you admire their success and ask them to share their story with you. You would be surprised at the number of people that will gladly share their story with you. Sometimes, these very people can help you unlock your dream. If you do not know them personally, read their life story or whatever information that you can find about them.

_____

_____

_____

_____

_____

_____

_____

_____

_____

_____

_____

_____

5. How likely are you to pursue this dream?

Note: If you are not willing to pursue this dream wholeheartedly then you may need to reevaluate your priorities.

_____
_____
_____
_____
_____
_____
_____
_____
_____
_____
_____
_____
_____
_____
_____
_____

6. What steps would you need to take to fulfill this dream ultimately?
Describe the steps that you can make right now to begin that journey. Who are the people that you need to talk to about this action? This particular question should cause you to brainstorm available resources, skills required, and type of education necessary. *Caution - at this stage, looking at all the requirements to get there could be a little overwhelming and cause you to shrink back in fear. Do not be afraid; you will be amazed at the help that comes your way once you have become focused.*

Let's talk about what you discovered. I call this exercise that you just completed "Dreaming Out Loud." Briefly list what you discovered and include any "aha" moments that occurred.

_____

_____

_____

_____

_____

_____

_____

_____

_____

_____

Who Are You?

Let's talk about you. Who are you and what is your mission in life?

1. Describe your passions. What makes you feel fulfilled? What makes you come alive?

These are all clues to who you really are and will help to understand your personal mission.

_____
_____
_____
_____
_____
_____
_____
_____
_____
_____
_____
_____
_____
_____
_____

2. List three things that you would like to be known for in your lifetime.

_____
_____
_____
_____
_____
_____
_____
_____
_____
_____
_____
_____
_____
_____
_____

3. What are your biggest pet peeves? Pet peeves are things that annoy you. For example, one of my pet peeves is when people are late starting meetings. Give an example or two of some of your pet peeves.

_____

_____

_____

_____

_____

_____

_____

_____

_____

_____

_____

_____

_____

_____

_____

_____

4. If you could change a few things about your life what would they be?

5. What type of people do you tend to admire who are "making it" in life? Why?

6. What would you do in life, if you knew that you could not fail?

_____
_____
_____
_____
_____
_____
_____
_____
_____
_____
_____
_____
_____
_____
_____
_____
_____

7. What type of success do you fantasize about often?

_____
_____
_____
_____
_____
_____
_____
_____
_____
_____
_____
_____
_____
_____
_____
_____
_____

8. What's important to you regarding family?

___

9. What's important to you regarding friends?

10. Complete this statement -

   If I had my way in life, everyone would

   _____.

11. If you were to give a message to the entire world that could help in life, what would it be?

   _____
   _____
   _____
   _____
   _____
   _____
   _____
   _____
   _____
   _____

Your answers to these prompts give clues to who you are and what's important to you.

Now we are ready to move to Part B – "Making the Dream a Reality."

Part B
Making the Dream a Reality

Now that you have worked through Part A let's look closer at your dreams. What have you identified that give you clues about your dream? Fulfilling your dreams seldom moves in a straight trajectory. By that I mean that it is not as easy as a 1-2-3 cakewalk. There will be challenges and obstacles along the way that will test your patience, endurance, and at times cause you to feel hopeless.

Think back to that watermelon seed that I mentioned in the previous section. There is a period in the seed's development that is called "dormancy." Dormancy simply means that it is not actively growing. That seed is alone in the darkness buried in the dirt. Oddly enough, this is one of the most crucial times in the life of the seed. You see there are nutrients in the dirt and darkness that begins to eat away the hard outer covering of the seed. Just when it seems that there will never be enough to move out of that darkness – the "let me out" begins to swell within the seed and push through the darkness in search of daylight.

There will be times in the pursuit of your dreams that you see, hear, and feel nothing in regards to fulfillment. No one notices anything special about you, others around you may not value you, and other people may just ignore you. One thing that you cannot afford to do is give up on you regardless of how far away you may seem to be from fulfilling your dream. These situations often help to develop an inner strength in you. It gives you an opportunity to grow and develop. It causes your "let me out" to get stronger and stronger and pushes you toward your purpose.

So let's take a minute and look at a few things. First, you will have challenges and opportunities to walk away because it just seems too hard. What are some problems that you are facing or have faced that has you tempted to walk away?

You may have even questioned, "What's the use?" Could it be that this may be some of the dirt that has to be thrown on you to cause you to want more?

Go ahead and list those challenges.

_____
_____
_____
_____
_____
_____
_____
_____
_____
_____
_____
_____

Next, let's focus on where you are right now. What's your current situation? How are others' lives better because of your presence? I would like to make a distinction here. When answering, "How are others' lives better because of your presence?" Some of you may feel that no one's life is better because of your presence. Not because you have done anything wrong, but because you feel unwelcome, unwanted, or as if your life doesn't matter. Let me encourage you that your life does matter and you may simply be in a "dormant" time because you have yet to tap into your purpose. That is what this is about, helping you to discover why you exist and causing you to succeed in what you do.

Depending on your current situation, these may be easy to answer, or they may be difficult to explain for various reasons. I want to encourage you with something. There may be times that you cannot answer these questions in the affirmative. What I mean is that you may feel that you have caused many people a great deal of heartache, pain, and grief. Even if that is the case, you can turn those things around if you are willing to keep moving towards progress. Remember in the opening paragraph of Part A where I told you that "people are so accustomed to getting everything done in an instant and seeking immediate results that they miss what develops into something powerful over time." It takes time and consistently doing things differently to get the desired result.

What's your current situation and how are people's lives better because of you?

_____

_____

_____

_____

Some of you have done some things that you know that you absolutely caused some major problems. You find yourself in a web of mess. The situation is so smelly and stinky, that you wonder, "How in the world can I survive this stuff?" I have great news for you. Even a little manure – also known as "boo-boo," can provide nutrients to the soil that will cause the "let me out!" in your seed to come forth. Here's an assignment for you.

Who have you hurt/disappointed the most and how can you make amends? How will making amends help you to get closer to your dream if you get those things right?

Note: some people that will never accept your apology and that's okay. Just make a conscious decision that you will not make those same mistakes again. Everyone will not like you, and some of them may never forgive you. Don't let those people define you.

_____

_____

_____

_____

_____

_____

_____

_____

_____

Do you remember the analogy that I used in Part A to describe what having a dream means? *Dreams are things that you know do not exist at the current time, are currently out of reach, but you hope and believe that they can come true.* Here's my question to you – what's your dream? We have already discussed your challenges. Let's push those to the side for a minute and move forward as if those challenges don't matter right now. We will revisit them later. What do you want to do in your life that is significant and what problems do you wish you could solve? These are all clues to that dream. Answer these two questions:

What do you want to do that is significant and what problems do you wish you could solve?

_____

_____

_____

_____

_____

_____

_____

_____

_____

_____

_____

_____

To get to the place that you just described, we have to take steps to get there in chunks. These small pieces are what I meant earlier when I said that "you can become exponentially better than what you are currently."

Let's talk. What one thing in your life needs to change the most?

_____

_____

_____

_____

_____

_____

_____

What stands in the way of making this change?

_____

_____

_____

_____

_____

How will you benefit by making this change?

_____

_____

_____

_____

_____

_____

_____

_____

How long do you think that it will take to make this change? Set a realistic goal here by positively saying what you will change and by when.

_____

_____

_____

_____

_____

Who do you know that can do what you want to change? List all the people that you know either personally or from afar. What can you learn from their experiences?

_____
_____
_____
_____
_____
_____
_____
_____
_____
_____
_____
_____
_____
_____
_____
_____
_____

Congratulations! If you have made it this far in the guide and you are still eager to move forward with fulfilling your goals and dreams you are well on your way. Use the information in this guide to help you move forward in your life and begin impacting those around you. They will be amazed at your progress and growth.

Do not forget that this process takes time, effort, and patience to become who you truly want to be in life. At times it will be hard, frustrating, and lonely but do not under any circumstances give up on your dream!

After all, YOU are "purposed" and will succeed at what you do.

The Purposed Group, LLC
Dr. Michael A. Winters, Founder & CEO

Dr. Michael A. Winters is passionate about helping people to reach their full potential. He is a motivational speaker, school district administrator, and certified life coach. His heart is to help people to walk through life knowing that "purposed people" exist for a reason and they succeed in what they do.

Dr. Winters is a graduate of Warren Central High School, Vicksburg, MS and Jackson State University, Jackson, MS. He has a Bachelor of Science degree in Elementary Education, Master of Science degree in Educational Administration, and a Doctor of Philosophy in Educational Administration. He resides in Vicksburg, MS with his beautiful wife, Kimberly. They have two adult children and a daughter-in-law, Mychal (his wife Maya) and Victoria.

For additional information visit
PurposedGroup.com

www.ingramcontent.com/pod-product-compliance
Lightning Source LLC
Chambersburg PA
CBHW070757050426
42452CB00010B/1870